Material Detectives: Soil

Let's Look at a Garden

Angela Royston

Heinemann Library
Chicago, Illinois

Customer Service   888-454-2279

Visit our website at www.heinemannlibrary.com

Printed and bound in China by South China Printing Company Limited
Photo research by Erica Newbery

10 09 08 07 06
10 9 8 7 6 5 4 3 2 1

Library of Congress Cataloging-in-Publication Data
Royston, Angela.
  Soil : let's look at a garden / Angela Royston.
      p. cm. -- (Material detectives)
  Includes index.
   ISBN 1-4034-7674-8 (lib. bdg. hardcover) -- ISBN 1-4034-7683-7 (pbk.)
  1. Garden soils--Juvenile literature. I. Title. II. Series: Royston, Angela. Material detectives.
   S596.75R77 2005
   631.4--dc22
                                                    2005004707

Acknowledgments
The author and publishers are grateful to the following for permission to reproduce copyright material:
Corbis p. 6; Digital Vision p. 19 (tiger); Ernie James/NHPA p. 8; George W Miller/Science Photo Library p. 5; Getty Images/Photodisc p. 19 (earthworm and fish); Harcourt Education pp. 14, 17, 22 (sand and soil), 23 (crack), 24; Holt Studios International 2003 p. 12; Holt Studios p. 21; Oxford Scientific p. 20; Paul Hobson/Alamy pp. backcover (mole), 18, 23 (tunnel); Photodisc pp. 4, 23 (plot); Photolibrary/Eric Kamp pp. backcover (boots), 13; Tudor Photography/Harcourt Education Ltd pp. 7, 9, 10, 11, 15, 16, 22 (concrete), 23 (concrete, crumbly, and wilting).

Cover photograph of flowers reproduced with permission of Flowerphotos.com

Every effort has been made to contact copyright holders of any material reproduced in this book. Any omissions will be rectified in subsequent printings if notice is given to the publisher.

Many thanks to the teachers, library media specialists, reading instructors, and educational consultants who have helped develop the Read and Learn/Lee y aprende brand.

Some words are shown in bold, **like this**. They are explained in the glossary on page 23.

Contents

What is a Garden?

A garden is a **plot** of soil.

People grow plants in a garden.

Soil holds the plants in place in the garden.

What is Soil?

Soil is a layer of earth.

Plants and some animals live in soil.

Soil feels **crumbly**.

It can make your hands dirty!

Why Do Plants Need Soil?

Soil gives plants water and food.

Most of the water comes from rain.

This soil is too dry and the plant is **wilting**.

What should you do?

You should pour more water onto the soil!

The plant takes in the water.

The plant soon begins to grow again.

What Kinds of Soil are There?

Some soil is very sandy and dry.

It blows around in the wind.

Some soil is wet and muddy.

It sticks to shoes and boots!

Where Do Flowers Grow Best?

Flowers grow best in soil that is not too sandy or too wet.

Can you grow flowers on **concrete**?

No, you cannot grow flowers on **concrete**!

They would die.

Some plants grow in the **cracks** in concrete.

They grow in the soil between the cracks.

What Animals Live in the Soil?

Moles live in the soil.

They dig **tunnels** to move around.

tiger

earthworm

fish

Which of these animals do you think lives in soil?

Earthworms live in the soil.

They eat fallen leaves.

Earthworms break up the soil.

They make it easier for plants to grow.

Quiz

Where do plants grow best?

Look for the answer on page 24.

sand

dark, **crumbly** soil

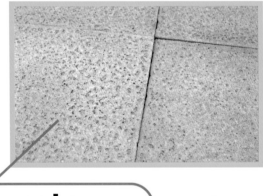

concrete

Glossary

concrete
material that looks like stone. It is made from a mixture of sand, gravel, cement, and water

crack
small gap

crumbly
breaks up easily

plot
marked out area

tunnel
hole underground

wilting
slowly drying up and falling over

Index

Answer to the quiz question on page 22

A plant would grow best in the dark, crumbly soil because it is not too wet or too dry.

Note to parents and teachers

Reading for information is an important part of a child's literacy development. Learning begins with a question about something. Help children think of themselves as investigators and researchers by encouraging their questions about the world around them. Each chapter in this book begins with a question. Read the question together. Look at the pictures. Talk about what you think the answer might be. Then read the text to find out if your predictions were correct. Think of other questions you could ask about the topic, and discuss where you might find the answers. Assist children in using the picture glossary and the index to practice new vocabulary and research skills.